CW01668761

Then & Now

Ramsgate

Then & Now
Ramsgate

Vince Runacre

The History Press

Frontispiece: Looking out over Ramsgate's Royal Harbour, comparing the view from 100 years ago and today.

First published 2008

The History Press Ltd.
Cirencester Road, Chalford,
Stroud, Gloucestershire, GL6 8PE
www.thehistorypress.co.uk

British Library Cataloguing in Publication Data.
A catalogue record for this book is available from the British Library.

ISBN 978 0 7524 4458 1

Typesetting and origination by The History Press Ltd.
Printed in Great Britain

Contents

Acknowledgements

Almost all of the original postcards within this book are from the personal collection of Richard and Janet Mason, which they built up at considerable expense. So by far the biggest thank you has to go to them for allowing me to reproduce their old postcards within this book, as without their permission to use these images this book would simply not have been possible.

Thanks also to Isobel Buck at Francis Frith for the necessary copyright approvals to reproduce the images owned by them, and to Fiona for her patience whilst putting this book together.

I would also like to thank Nicola Guy and the publishers at History Press for taking this idea and making it a reality.

Much of the research for this book has been taken from my personal experiences growing up in this town, and from the local stories and facts one picks up whilst spending many years in a particular place. There are a number of fine local history books and articles already published on Ramsgate, which have assisted me to fill in the blanks, so if you would like to learn more about this fascinating town, you really will be spoilt for choice!

An aerial photograph of Ramsgate as it is now. The approximate location of each chapter has been marked on this map. (*Image copyright © Microsoft, 2007. http://maps.live.com*)

Introduction

The town of Ramsgate began life as a small fishing and farming hamlet. Ramsgate as a name has its earliest reference as *Hraefn's Ate*, or cliff gap, later rendered 'Ramisgate' or 'Remmesgate' around 1225, and 'Ramesgate' from 1357. For centuries, however, some have insisted the name actually comes from 'Roman's-gate', and that Julius Casear first landed here and set up a fortified camp where the town is now before going on to conquer Britain.

Whatever its origins, Ramsgate has often played a front-line role in history. The Viking leaders Hengest and Horsa landed here in the fifth century, and the Christian missionary St Augustine also landed in Ramsgate in 597, marking the beginning of Christianity in England.

Due to its proximity to mainland Europe, the town was also a chief embarkation point both during the Napoleonic Wars and for the Dunkirk evacuation in 1940.

Many things have been written about the town of Ramsgate over the last couple of centuries, such as this from a nineteenth-century Victorian journal:

> The streets of Ramsgate are well paved or macadamised, and brilliantly lighted with gas. An excellent promenade on the West Cliff has been laid out in an ornamental manner, and forms a delightful source of healthy recreation. The bathing-machines are under the East Cliff where also, as well as in front of the harbour, there are well-appointed warm baths, etc.
>
> The markets are extremely well supplied with meat and excellent fish, and few places on the coast are so cheap, as well as healthy and agreeable for a summer's residence.
>
> We need not be surprised at the popularity which Ramsgate continues to enjoy as a watering place, when these and many other advantages present themselves for the convenience of the visitor.

However, opposite views were also common:

> It requires marvellous courage now to confess any interest in places so utterly discarded by fashion as is Ramsgate. It is still crowded, but by decidedly unfashionable and objectionable people.

Chronicles of Fashion by Elizabeth Stone (1845)

So what is the purpose of this book?

There are many excellent local history books already written about Ramsgate and its surrounding towns and villages, so why publish another one?

Well, this book is unique in using the popular 'Then and Now' format, using old postcards instead of photographs to show in an instant how time has visibly changed aspects of the town over the last century or more. Each view is a snapshot in time, where I have always tried to recapture the exact angle and view of a shot as seen in the original postcard. This often presented challenges and in some cases just was not possible as the building or vantage point where the original photographer had once stood is no longer there! But, for the most part, it was a strange feeling to be standing with my camera in the exact same spot where a Victorian or Edwardian photographer would have stood all those years ago.

I personally feel it is fascinating to study these contrasting views, to see not just what has changed in this busy seaside town, but also what has not. In over 100 years, some scenes are still identical, with the same buildings, scenery and character as a century ago, despite the ravages of time.

Over the years, Ramsgate, along with its sister towns of Margate and Broadstairs, has seen a lot of changes, perhaps not always with its scenery, but more often behind the scenes, such as in its economy and popularity.

Kent coastal towns like these really boomed during Victorian times, when British seaside resorts were much in vogue. But during the Second World War, it was, perhaps reluctantly, thrust to the foreground to play a key role as a front-line town in Kent's notorious 'hellfire corner'. Coastal defences lined the cliffs, beaches were fenced off, the town's young were evacuated en masse, and the remaining population spent much of their time hiding underground in Ramsgate's famous air-raid tunnels as the town endured almost daily bombardment from Hitler's forces.

After the Second World War ended, Ramsgate still remained popular throughout the fifties and sixties as a place to 'get away to', with train loads of excited tourists arriving from London and other areas to see the seaside. However, after the war it never quite regained its former sparkle and with the arrival of cheap package holidays abroad by the early seventies, like so many other coastal resorts, the town went into a slow decline. It needed to find its feet again and redefine its purpose.

Happily, today Ramsgate appears to be booming once again. With the prospect of a high-speed rail link to London, expansion of its airport and rising property prices, it has recently been labelled by the national press as a hot spot for investment.

As development in the town continues at a breathtaking rate, many feel it is important that the town still retains much of its earlier charm and character, as is so nicely portrayed in the old postcards within this book. There is no holding back progress, but my hope is that new development will be done in a sympathetic way, ensuring that the heritage, character and visual history of this marvellous town is preserved for future generations, as it has been (for the most part) up to now.

As I stated earlier, this book is simply to show the town as it was during its Victorian heyday and the same view today. Where possible, I have tried to include some historical facts or other points of interest in the related captions.

All the modern photographs were taken by myself on my compact digital camera. For me it was not about taking professional style photographs – I just wanted a simple snapshot of the same view to show the reader instantly how it now appears rather than using fancy lighting or timed exposures. However, what this book does is bring the two strands together in what I believe to be an effective mix of history and pictures.

As someone who was brought up in Ramsgate, and still lives here, I have many happy memories in this town and a great affection for it, so this book was important to me and I really hope I have done the town some justice.

I've enjoyed putting this book together and I hope you enjoy it too!

Vince Runacre
February 2008

1

The Town

Located seventy-eight miles south-east of London, and with a population of 40,000 inhabitants, the coastal town of Ramsgate is one of the most easterly points in the country. It is actually an amalgamation of two original settlements – a fishing community on the coast, and a farming community further inland (known as the parish of St Laurence). The town remains an exciting tourist resort with an eclectic mix of Georgian, Regency and Victorian buildings.

St George's Church, *c.* 1895. This building, with its impressive neo-gothic architecture, still dominates the Ramsgate skyline today. The church was consecrated in 1827. Its tower is topped with an impressive octagonal stone lantern, which was added at the request of Trinity House (the lighthouse authority) to act as a navigational aid to passing ships. This has recently been renovated at a cost of over £1.2 million. Restoration work began in January 2001 and finished in September 2004. Each face of the lantern bears a letter spelling St George and the weathervane on top has a bullet hole in it that was collected during the Second World War. Inside is the famous Dunkirk Window, a stained-glass window commemorating the evacuation of Dunkirk in 1940. Actor John LeMesurier (of BBC's *Dad's Army* fame), was buried here in 1983.

The main precinct in Ramsgate High Street, *c.* 1905 and today. This is the main crossroads in the centre of the precinct, with Harbour Street straight ahead, King Street to the left and Queen Street to the right. The original building on the right with the pillared frontage was once the Town Hall (erected in 1839), but is now the Halifax Building Society, with the front facade having been redeveloped, minus the attractive pillars. Page & Sons is now the Harbour Street Bar.

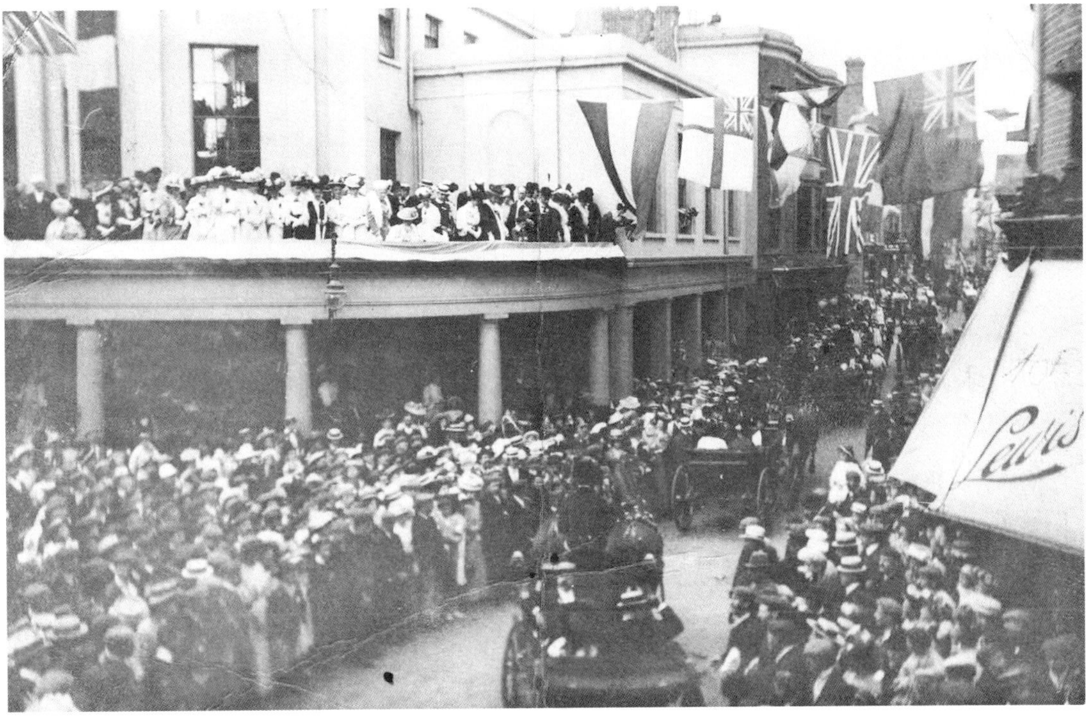

The original picture was taken during the 'French Visit' of 6 August 1907. This occasion no doubt provided a great source of excitement and interest to the local residents, with many hundreds turning out in their 'Sunday best' to welcome the visiting French dignitaries as they paraded through the town. The pillared building on the left is now the Halifax Building Society. As in the previous picture, the frontage has changed significantly, but this distinctive corner building, which also used to house the council chambers, is still recognisable. I think these days the Health and Safety Executive would have something to say about that crowd of people standing on the roof with no safety railings!

A view looking down Vale Road, taken at the turn of the twentieth century, and today. The Vale Tavern has remained a popular watering hole since 1867, when Henry Laslett was the original landlord. Vale Road was also home in 1903 to Mr George Lawrence, a well-known bathing-machine proprieter who lived at number seven. The scene has not really changed that much in over 100 years, except for the obvious addition of motor cars. Can you see any more changes? Play 'spot the difference'!

J. & T. Turner. 50 Plains of Waterloo, Ramsgate. First Class Fruiterers.

Plains of Waterloo, 1905 and today. Number fifty is still a grocery store, over 100 years later, and as you can see, very little has changed in its external appearance. The interesting name for this street dates back to the Regency period of the early 1800s, when many troops were billetted in Ramsgate, ready to cross the channel to fight Napoleon's forces. Several streets of fine Georgian houses were constructed on the east side of the Harbour, originally to serve as officer's accommodation. Nearby roads also tell similar tales of Ramsgate's role as a front-line garrison town during the Napoleonic Wars, with names such as La Belle Alliance Square, Nelson Crescent and Artillery Road.

Spencer Square around 1900 and today. The original bowling green is now tennis courts. Carlton House was originally a YMCA hostel in the early picture, but is now a private residence, currently with scaffolding along the front. Other than the new pavillion and refreshments building not much else has changed, probably because most of these buildings are Grade II listed.

During 1876, Vincent Van Gogh boarded here, at number eleven Spencer Square, whilst he worked as a supply teacher at a school in nearby Royal Road. He even made some sketches of the view from these lodgings, overlooking the harbour.

St Mildred's Road around 1900 and today. This pleasant tree-lined road has many impressive Regency properties. It is nice to see that over a century later many of the trees still remain. Obvious changes in the modern view include the addition of cars, lining both sides of the road. St Mildred's Road connects the High Street in Grange Road with the busy London Road, leading out of Ramsgate. Walking along St Mildred's Road today, it is quite striking to see all the different styles of buildings from one house to the next, a kind of architectural patchwork from many different decades.

St Lawrence High Street around 1905 and today. The differences between these two scenes are quite dramatic. The entire row of buildings on the right-hand side were demolished many years ago to enable the road to be widened so as to cope with increasing traffic demands. A petrol station and post office now stand in their place, with newer houses set further back. The fronts of the original terraced buildings would have been where the hatching is in the middle of the road in the new picture. This starkly represents the high cost of progress, as this quaint little High Street has reluctantly become one of the main arterial roads leading into and out of Ramsgate. You can also just make out the Wheatsheaf pub in the middle of the picture (behind the white road sign), which was originally painted pink in the earlier view.

Number six Albion Hill in 1915, and the same view today. The original photo shows the Imperial Bazaar in Albion Hill after it was bombed during a Zeppelin airship raid at the height of the First World War. This was likely to have been one of the first times the town had ever experienced an aerial bombardment, judging by the look of wonderment on some of the local people's faces. The stern police constable is proudly performing his duty and keeping the onlookers back! Not surprisingly, the damage has long since been repaired, and the building is now a private residence.

Grange Road, *c*.1905. Note the windmill in the centre of the picture on the left side of the road. The windmill was one of several in Ramsgate, and was demolished in 1930. Standing on the corner of Cannonbury Road and Grange Road, it had a fascinating history. It was originally built on the East Cliff but was later dismantled and erected on this site in 1810. It was last used in 1913 and partially demolished in 1927. The base was then used as a garage before being completely demolished three years later. The site is now a Chinese restaurant.

The old Ramsgate Town Station around 1900, and the same site today.

In the mid-1800s, the old windmills on this site were pulled down to make way for the original railway station which was located at the top of Margate Road, next to the Hovis Mill site.

During the First World War the station received a direct hit from a Zeppelin air raid and was never used again. In 1926 McAlpine built the railway from Margate to Canterbury and a new town station was constructed about half a mile away. This old station then lay derelict for many years.

After the Second World War the site was eventually cleared and the existing Chatham Court flats were built in its place. The gardens of the houses on Station Approach Road are now where the old railway track used to be, and the old railway embankment can still be clearly seen behind them.

Ramsgate Mill in 1900 and today. Situated next door to the old town station (on the previous page), this building was owned by Hudsons and was once a hive of activity and a major local employer, as well as being a prime target for German bombs during both World Wars. The additional frontage to the main building (the screen room) in the modern view was constructed in the early 1900s and the large grain silo to the left was built in 1935. The site was closed in 2005 as Rank Hovis deemed it was no longer commercially viable. It has now been sold to a private developer and work has begun to convert it into luxury housing. The main building is Grade II Listed, so it is likely that at least the original façade will remain.

Ramsgate Library in 1904 and the remains of it in 2007. The grand building which was Ramsgate Library was built in 1904 from a generous donation made to the town by Andrew Carnegie, a Scottish-American steel tycoon. The original postcard shows it during winter. The park in the original picture vanished a long time ago, and has since been built over with houses, as can be seen in the modern photo. Sadly, only a few months away from its centenary, the library was almost completely destroyed by an arson attack in August 2004, with only the Edwardian façade remaining. Fire crews from many neighbouring towns fought valiantly against the blaze, but the fire was so fierce they even had to draw water from the inner harbour basin to tackle the blaze. When the flames were finally doused, little was left of the building but a shell. Fortunately, plans to rebuild the library are progressing well.

Harbour Street in 1900 and today. Harbour Street connects Ramsgate Harbour with the Town Centre and is a fascinating street, as well as being one of the oldest in the town. Looking at the two views here, many of the original shop fronts still remain, albeit with different uses, and at first glance very little has changed. However, in keeping up with Ramsgate's prevailing 'café culture', at the time of writing there were no less than twelve cafés and restaurants in Harbour Street, so certainly no shortage of choice (or food) in a street just 400ft long!

High Street around 1905 and today. This view is taken from the top of the main High Street, looking down towards the harbour. Fine Regency buildings stand either side of the precinct. There is also a street market here every Friday and Saturday. There is an early motor car in the earlier picture, but today it is pedestrianised. The buildings, although the same, always appear a lot grander in the original pictures, with everybody smartly dressed, and the gentlemen wearing their boater hats. What was the parcels office in the original picture is now a high-street jewellers, with the main post office now situated just across the road.

ABERDEEN HOUSE, RAMSGATE.

Aberdeen House, around 1907 and today. This elegant Victorian building in Ellington Road is full of charm and character and was originally built as a boarding school for boys in the 1880s, when it had a total of nine pupils! The schoolmaster at that time was the Revd George Simmers. By the early twentieth century it became a boarding house, owned by Miss A. Simmers (presumably his daughter). It is now owned by Kent County Council and for many years has served as Ramsgate's Registry Office.

Bellevue Road around 1905 and today. An attractive view looking down Bellevue Road. Over a century later, many of the shop fronts still remain as they were, although some have since been converted into residential flats and bed sits. Trams would trundle along this road, on their way down Madeira Walk to the seafront, and they would certainly have been a familiar sight right up until the 1930's and the arrival of the motor bus.

A billboard outside the tobacconists can be seen in the original picture, loudly advertising the latest 'Penny Shockers', the predecessor of today's tabloids.

Ramsgate High Street, 1915 and today. A slightly more recent picture now, taken of the Bull & George public house in Ramsgate's town centre, after it was wrecked by German bombs from a Zeppelin air raid on 17 May 1915. This pub and hotel was one of the oldest in Ramsgate, and twelve people died when it took a direct hit. The pub was subsequently demolished, and a Woolworths store was built in its place around 1920. Woolworths is still there (to the right of the modern picture) as well as some newer-style shops on the site where the old Bull & George used to be.

2

Ramsgate Sands

I think there is no more amusing sight, at the height of the season, than the Ramsgate sands. There you can see thousands of people ... enjoying themselves. The fun is all very quiet and harmless, and all participate in it, from the youngest to the eldest. By the way, it is always the man who carries the baby, or wheels the perambulator, in accordance, I presume, with the theory that the woman is the weaker vessel.

Round London : Down East and Up West, by Montagu Williams Q.C., 1894

The Main Sands at Ramsgate, around 1908. The domed structure on the left is the top of an Edwardian lift shaft, leading down to the main sands. This was the first lift to be installed in Ramsgate, and it has recently been refurbished and re-opened by Thanet District Council after years of dereliction. It is now open for business throughout the summer season. There were many forms of entertainment plying their trade along the beach at this time such as donkey rides, folk selling toffee apples, photographers and engravers, and of course the ever-present Punch & Judy shows.

Main Sands and the Pavillion, *c.* 1905. Ramsgate was an extremely popular holiday destination during the Victorian and Edwardian eras, with train loads of excited day trippers all making the journey from London. An extract from a letter written in Victorian times gives a flavour for what it was like:

'Today I have had such an amazing day. Papa and Mama took the whole family to the beach at Ramsgate! Yes, all that way and we went by train. Mother was shocked at father's suggestion that he might nude bathe with the other men at their separate area of the beach. She suggested that a bathing machine might be more appropriate.

The beach was already quite crowded but we found a place to establish ourselves and when the chairs arrived all was complete. Father had paid to have them fetched from a nearby hotel. We girls were content to promenade along the sand, watching a Punch and Judy show and listened to the hurdy gurdy player. We held our parasols aloft and our bonnets in place to keep the sun from reaching us. Indeed, had it not been for the gloves we had brought, I fear that we might have had very pink hands by the end of the day! Ramsgate itself is a fine town and we finished off our day with a tray of tea at a tea shop on the promenade.'

The bathing machines are notably absent from the recent picture though!

The 'New' Pavilion in 1906 and the same view today. Originally the Pavilion contained many shops including a photographic studio, as well as a tea room and other refreshments. The Royal Pavilion was built in 1904 and opened by Princess Louise, the second-youngest daughter of Queen Victoria. After a brief period in the 1980s and 1990s as a nightclub, the pavilion is now the Grosvenor Casino, but externally it has changed very little.

The East Pier of the Royal Harbour can be seen in the background, and also the tall, pointed structure to the right is an obelisk erected to mark King George IV's visit to the town in 1821, and is nicknamed the Royal Toothpick!

View from the Pavilion, 1905. Standing outside the Pavilion, this view is looking across the inner basin of the harbour towards the town and shows a nice view of the buildings which would give mariners their first view of the town. A fascinating mix of achitectural styles can be seen when looking at the properties lining the seafront.

View of the old Ramsgate Harbour (or Sands) Station, around 1905 and 2008. This was the site of a once-bustling railway station, which first opened on 5 October 1863 by the London, Chatham & Dover Railway. Passengers were able to disembark right on the sands of Ramsgate's main beach. The station closed in July 1926 along with Ramsgate Town Station (page 21) after the various railway companies were amalgamated into the Southern Railway. The Harbour Station building remained, however, and was converted into a large amusement arcade and funfair called Merrie England, which was later renamed 'Pleasurama'. Many residents, myself included, spent much of our youth in that old station building, playing video games and pool. This characteristic building was sadly razed to the ground in an arson attack in the late 1990s. As can be seen in the modern picture, this site is currently being redeveloped into a luxury housing and leisure complex. It is also incredible to see in the original postcard how crowded the beach once was!

The Promenade, Ramsgate Sands, around 1904. Tucked behind the lifeguard station in the modern view, you can still see the Marina Restaurant, also visible in the original postcard. After serving more recently as a café, this old building later became derelict. In February 2008 most of the building had to be demolished, although it should soon be rebuilt just as it was, due to its Listed status. As you can see in the original postcard, the sands were a hive of activity at the turn of the twentieth century, with bathing-machine proprieters and deckchair vendors mingling with the many residents and holidaymakers all out for a stroll, just for the sheer enjoyment of it. Also prominent in the old view was the Marina Pleasure Pier, which opened in 1881 and was 550ft long. It survived several accidents in its time including ship collisions, fires and exploding mines, before finally being demolished in 1930. However, at low tide, the remains of the original struts can still be seen where it once stood.

Kent Terrace, around 1903 and today. These two views are striking in their similarity showing how little has changed in over a century! A large part of the chalk cliff was dug away in order to build Kent Terrace.

The arcade of original restaurants (in the foreground) is now an amusement arcade. In the original postcard, the large restaurant on the far left was aptly called 'G. James's Victoria Dining Rooms' and offered such traditional fayre as 'Sausage, Mash & Onions' and 'Fish Suppers'. According to its sign, 'School Parties' were also catered for, apparently! Kent Terrace was named in honour of the Duchess of Kent, who was a frequent visitor to the town.

This view of the main sands shows just how busy they were in their Victorian heyday. Holidaymakers crammed into any space available, and lines of bathing machines dominated the shoreline at the water's edge. The resident 'puppet show' can be seen as the main attraction; in this case it was 'Dugwell's famous Marionettes'. It may seem strange today to see everybody in the original picture enjoying the sun fully clothed, but apart from that, they do seem to be relaxing on the beach in much the same way as we would today, over 100 years later. As you can see in the modern picture, the sands seem a lot quieter, however at peak season the crowds are still returning to Ramsgate.

Ramsgate Sands paddling area, around 1905 and today. Although most of the time the crowds have gone, and the windows of the Pavilion are now blocked up, this area still remains a pleasant place to sit and watch the sea, although very little paddling happens here now. The whole Pavilion is now the Grosvenor Casino. Nowadays, the local council face a running battle with graffiti artists in this particular area who are constantly 'tagging' the walls of this once great pavillion.

Sands and Pavilion, around 1910 and today. Here the grand-looking pavilion is decked out as a marquis on the upper level, with some flags flying above it. The large Edwardian crowd are intently staring out to sea – perhaps they are watching one of the regular sailing regattas taking place. The beach is clearly more deserted in the modern picture, probably because this photo was taken during the winter. Like many others, this picture really demonstrates the attitudes and customs of the time – the adults are all fully clothed, even wearing hats and jackets. The young children, however, seem to be happily running around in just a pair of shorts or bathing costume. Nowadays almost everyone would be wearing far less on the beach during summer and would not give it a second thought!

Ramsgate Sands and Railway Station, around 1906, and same view in 2007. Note the missing railway station in the modern view, which burned down in the late 1990s after it was used as an amusement arcade for many decades. The chalk cliffs in the background have also since been reinforced by concrete. The attractive row of Georgian houses dominating the skyline is known as Wellington Crescent.

Interestingly, in the earlier picture, rather than deckchairs there appears to be what look like several park benches on the sand! Note again the adults paddling in the sea, still fully clothed!

3

The Harbour

Designed by Smeaton and Rennie, the two big names in Georgian marine engineering, Ramsgate's Royal Harbour has changed little since 1793. It played a leading role in both the Napoleonic Wars and 'Operation Dynamo', the legendary evacuation of British troops stranded on the beaches of Dunkirk in the Second World War.

This is another contrast of two views a century apart. The old photograph shows Harbour Parade as it was in 1901. Not a great deal has changed in all this time, except the mode of public transport. Buses continue to stop outside the Royal public house, in the same spot as the trams did a century ago. And prior to the trams, horse-drawn charabancs would often queue here in the late nineteenth century, to collect fare-paying passengers and take them on popular sightseeing excursions. Looking at the bollards in the foreground, it is clear to see how the Parade has been extended out into the Harbour basin in the recent view.

Inner Harbour in 1860. This photograph shows a very early view of the inner harbour basin near the entrance to Harbour Street, with Albion Place behind. The Royal Clarence Baths on the left are now Harvey's Pub and Restaurant. As with the picture on the previous page, the road has evidently since been widened, reclaiming some of the inner harbour, when the 'new' approach road was constructed at the turn of the twentieth century. In addition, the Royal Albion Hotel, in the centre of the old picture, was half demolished in 1892 to make way for the construction of Madeira Walk, which was quite literally hewn out of the chalk behind it (a bus can be seen in the modern picture emerging from there). In later years, what was left of the Albion Hotel became the Natwest Bank, which has now been converted into a Pizza Express restaurant. The building on the far right of the upper level (with the flag pole) is Albion House, the Mayoral residence. Princess Victoria also stayed here on several occasions when visiting the town, prior to becoming Queen.

York Terrace and The Arcade in 1899. The Royal Temple Yacht Club is top left, having been established in Ramsgate since 1897. This pleasant little arcade of shops and restaurants still remains very popular today, as it was back then. The various restaurants here provide a taste of cuisine from all over the world, including Thai, Indian, Spanish and French. Walking down these steps towards The Arcade from Royal Parade provides a most spectacular view of Ramsgate Harbour and the seafront, which is beautifully lit up at night. Perhaps with a little imagination you could almost feel like you were in St Tropez or Monte Carlo on a warm summer evening!

East Pier, around 1890 and today. This view was taken halfway along the East Pier of the Royal Harbour, looking back towards Ramsgate. Considering all the decades that have since passed, and the many hundreds of bombs and shells that landed on this front-line town during two world wars, it is fascinating to see how the skyline of the town remains almost identical after a century. There are a few gaps here and there where buildings are now missing, perhaps destroyed by bombs or fire, but on the whole, this picture postcard scene remains unchanged.

Ramsgate Dry Dock (ship repair yard), around 1900 and today. The Dry Dock was built by John Smeaton in 1791. Again, these two views are very similar, albeit with a different ship in the dry dock undergoing repairs! The famous Maritime Museum is on the left, which contains many interesting exhibits of maritime history. This Grade II Listed Clock House was originally built in 1817 as a harbour office, containing an astronomical clock and meridian line for ships to set their instruments by. The clock was originally set to 'Ramsgate Mean Time', which was in fact five minutes and forty-one seconds ahead of Greenwich!

The Harbour Front around 1901 and today. The Alexandria Restaurant still remains, to the right of what was the Castle Hotel (now the Atlantis bar and restaurant). However, as can be seen, the Alexandria restaurant building is now set further back, no longer flush with the building next door, and has a somewhat 'Art Deco' exterior. Both these buildings date back as far as 1770, perhaps even earlier.

West Pier, around 1895 and today. The famous lighthouse at the end of the pier is still in use today. It was built from Portland Stone in 1843, and has the Latin words *perfugium miseris* cut into the stone below the lantern, which means 'shelter for the distressed'.

The *Royal Soverign* was a grand steamship built in 1892, owned by the VSA (Victorian Steamboat Association). It sailed regularly from its pier in central London to Southend, Essex and Kent seaside resorts, and was a frequent visitor to Ramsgate. This steamship, along with its two sisters, far surpassed the standards of all other Thames steamers at the time, and for many years to come. It stopped service at the outbreak of the First World War and was sold in 1918, never to be seen in these waters again. It obviously captured everyone's interest as it steamed gracefully past the pier into Ramsgate's inner harbour.

Harbour Approach and the 'New Road' around 1903 and today. Not very much has changed here, except for the construction of the Kent International Hotel (right of the modern picture), and more traffic of course! The motor car shown in the original picture would have been quite a rarity at that time, and no doubt received lots of stares from envious pedestrians!

Ramsgate Harbour played a leading role in 'Operation Dynamo', the famous evacuation of Dunkirk. In May 1940, a hastily assembled fleet of almost 900 fishing boats and pleasure cruisers sailed from Ramsgate Harbour to rescue thousands of British troops who were stranded on the beaches of Dunkirk, France. This curious assortment of little ships, many of which were privately owned, bravely sailed to and fro across the channel to rescue over 380,000 troops from the shores of Dunkirk, many of which were brought back to Ramsgate. Winston Churchill called it 'a miracle of deliverance', and for many of these exhausted and battle-weary soldiers, Ramsgate Harbour would certainly have been a comforting site, and their first view of home. One of these legendary 'little ships' is still moored in the inner harbour today.

Inner harbour in 1901 and today. Back in 1703, a violent storm almost wrecked an entire naval fleet which had been sheltering in the channel, near to the Goodwin Sands. Following that disastrous event, it was decided to build a safe refuge, or harbour, at Ramsgate. Construction of Ramsgate Harbour started in 1749 but apparently took over a century until it was finally completed. It gained its 'Royal' title in 1821 when King George IV visited here on an inspection of the Royal Yacht Squadron. He was so impressed by the warm welcome he received from the locals that he denominated Ramsgate a Royal harbour. As such, it is the only Royal harbour in the United Kingdom.

4

Ellington Park

Ellington Park is a beautiful public park in the centre of Ramsgate. It was once the site of a fifteenth-century manor house which had a very murky past! The park opened in 1893, with the picturesque grounds laid out by Cheal & Son. As can be seen in the following postcards, it also had many attractive Edwardian features, although sadly only the bandstand still remains today.

58 RAMSGATE. — Ellington Park. — LL.

This view from 1901 shows 'The Terrace', which was built atop the foundations of the old Ellington Manor House. In 1648, the manor house was the home of the notorious Adam Sprackling, who was hanged for the gruesome murder of his wife, who he killed on this very spot. In the years that followed their deaths, many claimed the mansion was haunted by their ghosts, so much so that the house was exorcised in 1730. Often ghostly hooves could be heard galloping through these grounds at night, although on further investigation, it was in fact discovered to be the noise coming from real horses at the nearby farm stables, being amplified and echoing through the caves and cellars beneath the park. However, because of its dark history, the manor house was eventually demolished, and in 1892 the grounds were sold to the Ramsgate Corporation for £12,000. On 7 September 1893, it re-opened as Ellington Park. In the modern view, railings still trace along the shape of the old manor house, and the original flint walls of the old house's basement can still be clearly seen, along with two interesting stones set within them, showing the Sprackling 'cross keys' symbol, and the years 1647 and 1649. A childhood story was that if these stone plaques were ever removed, it would unlock the evil within the house. Sadly someone obviously believed it, as these stones have recently been hacked away.

This attractive ornamental fountain was installed back in 1895 as a gift from a Mrs Barber and was donated in memory of her son. Sadly, it was demolished many decades ago and a bowling green now stands in its place behind the railings in the modern view. The bandstand is shrouded behind the trees in the modern picture, but remains very much in the same place as in the original postcard! The park's well laid out grounds remain very picturesque to this day.

The Bandstand in 1901 and today. This wonderful Edwardian bandstand really is the central attraction within the park, and would have hosted many fine musical performances throughout the decades, particularly in the 1920s and 1930s. Nowadays it is still very much intact, but rarely used for anything other than a meeting place for local youths to hang out and practice their latest skateboarding tricks!

Old Lake in the Park in 1901 and today. Originally, there was an attractive lake and fish pond in the park, straddled by a wooden bridge, as shown in the original postcard. Sadly this was filled in many years ago, and a large rockery now stands in its place. During the summer months the outline of the original pond can still be seen in the dry grass.

This rockery that can be seen in the modern picture is actually made from an artificial material called Pulhamite. Artificial rockeries made from this strange sandstone mix have appeared all over Ramsgate since about the 1890s with perhaps the most famous example being that of Madeira Walk (page 80).

Two more historic scenes from the park showing another view of the fountain and the fish pond from around 1904.

5

The West Cliff

From caves to concert halls, motor museums to monkey sanctuaries, and even one of the country's largest model villages, there was certainly no shortage of variety at Ramsgate's West Cliff! An attractive area to relax and take a stroll, the West Cliff remains one of the most scenic areas of the town.

Westcliff Promenade around 1895 and 2006. The Victorian shelter in the original postcard has since been replaced by a café/snack bar. The top entrance of a lift shaft can be seen in the modern picture, built in 1929. The open land to the left is known as 'Government Acre', which was apparently used as a parade ground for troops garrisoned in Ramsgate during the early nineteenth century. The original stones marking the boundary of this acre can still be seen. The Westcliff is a peaceful, scenic area of Ramsgate, and has changed very little over the last century.

The Westcliff Bandstand around 1895 and 2006. The original postcard was taken from a top-floor window of the Churchill Tavern and School of English across the street. The modern photograph was taken from a different elevation. The terrace of regal houses in the original picture later became the Regency Hotel and then the Regency School of English. Sadly, these listed buildings over time went into decline, most being used as temporary housing and bedsits. However they are now being redeveloped as luxury housing. The Bandstand has since completely vanished (like so many others), and the structure in the foreground of the modern picture is the now derelict Motor Museum, which prior to that was the West Cliff Hall, a concert venue which hosted many famous bands throughout the years, including The Beatles and The Rolling Stones.

St Lawrence Bandstand, Westcliff, 1905 and today. This is the second bandstand that used to be situated on the Westcliff. Many decades ago, the bandstand disappeared, and became a boating lake. The site remains almost unchanged, except now it is full of water! The crescent-shaped buildings also remain intact, and actually became a monkey sanctuary during the 1980s. The main building is still a cafeteria, with a children's play park and art gallery also on the site today.

Westcliff Lawns, early 1900s and today. Again, this earlier picture was taken before the lift was built, from the promenade to the Western under-cliff. Again, the bandstand shown in the old view on page 58 has since been replaced with a shelter in this postcard, which in more recent times has been converted into a cafe/snack bar. The alleyway behind the shelter is known as 'Screaming Alley' which apparently got its name during the Napoleonic Wars of the early 1800s. According to local legend, many ladies of the town would walk back up this alley each night after visiting the naval officers stationed in the area. When returning up this alley they would usually be rather merry (as well as slightly intoxicated), laughing and shrieking and making a great deal of noise!

Nelson Crescent, Westcliff, 1895 and today. Very little has changed here in over a century. Except for the Victorian lamp posts being replaced with the Edwardian style ones, and of course the inevitable addition of cars. This was once a very regal area of Ramsgate, with the fine Regency buildings being constructed in the early 1800s as accommodation for the British naval officers, who were billetted in the town during the Napoleonic Wars.

St Augustine's Abbey, 1900 and today. This Grade I Listed Roman Catholic church was designed in the Victorian Gothic style by the well-known architect Augustus Welby Pugin, and built in 1844. It is linked by an underground tunnel to the monastery across the road, which was built by Pugin's son Edward in 1860, and is home to an order of Benedictine monks. Next door to this church is another famous Pugin building called The Grange. Finally completed in 1850, Pugin went on to live at The Grange until his death two years later. These buildings marked a break from the usual Regency style of the period, and went on to be very influential in the development of British architecture of the time. The Grange was purchased by the Landmark Trust in 1997 and restored back to how it was in Pugin's day. Its renovation was featured as a *Time Team Special* programme on television. Note the two lion statuettes above the gate of the abbey – see if you can spot similar statues in another picture of a famous Pugin building, elsewhere in this book.

Western undercliff, 1895 and today. The original view, with its Victorian shelters and ornamental planters, show this was once a very popular place to promenade or just relax in tranquil surroundings. Most of the western undercliff has been extensively redeveloped during the last decade to make way for a road access link connecting the port with the motorway via an underground tunnel, which runs inland from the Westcliff. The entrance to the road tunnel, which now dominates much of the western undercliff, is just to the left of this photograph. In 1947 much of the chalk cliff collapsed here after a spell of particularly severe weather. These cliffs had already been severely weakened by a warren of catacombs and tunnels which Pugin had excavated whilst living at 'The Grange'. They became known as St Augustine's caves, and were used in both world wars as air-raid shelters. They even contained an underground ballroom! Now large concrete arches (built to shore up the cliff) cover the entrances to what is left of this tunnel system.

6

Pegwell Bay

The historic home of shrimping and smuggling, rugged Pegwell Bay with its quaint village is an oasis of calm with a rich historic past. Throughout the 1820s many people watched regattas here under the patronage of Earl Darnley, when purses of gold sovereigns were given as prizes to the participants in yacht races.

Many famous visitors to Pegwell in the nineteenth century included Queen Victoria and Charles Dickens, who came to sample the famous shrimp paste, shrimp teas, and shrimp anything really!

Ye Olde Pegwell Bay (Nr. Ramsgate)

Pegwell Bay is one of the most scenic and interesting areas along the Kent Coast. Rugged and wild, the coastline around this pretty bay has seen a lot of changes over the centuries, along with the constant erosion of its chalk cliffs. Its name has also changed several times, having previously been known as Hope Bay, Courtstairs Bay and Greystone Bay. Now a peaceful haven for wildlife and nature, Pegwell Bay was very popular during Victorian and Edwardian times as a bustling holiday spot, with tea rooms, bathing facilities and regular regattas on offer. The picture above was drawn in the early nineteenth century, before the Belle Vue Hotel, with its prominent tower, was built in 1897. Note the two covered piers or jetties, extending out to sea. In front of these are wooden stumps of an earlier pier, built in 1784. These wooden posts can still be seen today jutting out of the sea at low tide. The inset picture shows a bait digger on the sands of the bay in the early 1900s, much the same as you see today.

Compared to the earlier picture on the previous page, in this old photograph (taken early 1900s) the piers and bathing facilities have now disappeared, and the Belle Vue Hotel has been built, with its characteristic tower. This building was originally the Clifton Hotel, and then became the Working Men's Club and Institute Union Convalescent Home. It has recently been renovated, and the Belle Vue Hotel (or Pegwell Bay Hotel as it is now called) is once again a popular place to stay. Compared with the modern view, the four-storey Conyngham Hotel in the foreground of the early photo has now completely disappeared, although the building next to it (partially obscured) is still there, forming part of the Pegwell Bay Hotel complex. Also the neatly manicured lawns in the foreground of the original picture have now become overgrown and wild. The concrete cliff reinforcements are also clearly seen in the recent picture, which were not present on previous ones.

The Sportsman Inn around 1910 and today. Not much has changed here, other than the type of transport in the car park, in addition to the newer houses on the left and an extension to the pub on the right (partially shown). The Sportsman has been a popular pub for well over 160 years. Back in 1847, a Mr George Williams was the proprietor.

Pegwell Bay and Gardens, around 1900 and today. This view again shows the four-storey Conyngham Hotel & Restaurant building in front of the cliff (now demolished), along with its extensive and well-laid-out gardens, originally known as Ravens Cliff Gardens. These nicely arranged lawns, along with the Conyngham Hotel, were built on land reclaimed from the bay, which prior to that was an open-air bathing pool. The modern view shows the land as it is now, (looking in the opposite direction). These once-landscaped gardens are now completely overgrown and wild, showing over the years how nature has reclaimed them back!

Pegwell Village around 1895 and today. The Belle Vue Tavern can be seen clearly on the left, and what is now the Sir Stanley Grey public house is next door. Previously this pub was called the Moonlighters after its extensive smuggling connections. There are numerous smuggling caves and tunnels that run from beneath the village, through the chalk cliffs to the sea. The building straight ahead (in the old picture) is the top floor of what used to be the Conyngham Hotel. There was also a large

flight of wooden steps which led down the cliff face to the beach below, and served as a lookout tower for the coastguard station. These wooden steps can still be seen today, over 100 years later, within the beer garden of the Belle Vue Tavern.

The building on the right, with the hoardings, was the Banger Brothers' Shrimp Factory, which served everything from shrimp teas to shrimp paste, to a discerning Victorian crowd, including visiting royalty. Prior to that it was the Pear Tree Inn.

Assumption Convent, Chilton, around 1895 and the convent site in 2006. In 1891, Convent of the Assumption was a Catholic boarding school for girls which had around twenty pupils. It later relocated to Sidmouth in Devon, and the Convent building was demolished many years ago, with a new housing estate springing up in its place. The only prominent feature that still remains of the convent is the original archway, on Goodwin Road (shown on the left of both pictures) and the 'Nun's Graveyard', located near the adjacent Convent Walk. The whole site is now a housing estate with several new roads and streets intersecting it.

7

The East Cliff

*H*ome to many fine Regency and Victorian buildings, Ramsgate's impressive East Cliff has a very rich history, and gives some fine views out to sea, across the treacherous Goodwin Sands.

East Cliff Promenade in 1905 and 2007. It is nice to see that the original Victorian shelters still remain, and have recently had a touch of paint. Like so many other bandstands across Ramsgate, this one has also disappeared as newer forms of entertainment take their place. There were once several bandstands situated along Ramsgate seafront in the early twentieth century, from the end of the West Cliff all the way along to the East Cliff, as well as in most of the parks. Some do still remain, but not many. Behind the Victorian shelter in the original postcard you can see Coastguard Cottages, built by the Admiralty in 1860.

Also in the earlier picture you may just be able to make out the dome of another lift shaft that went from the sea front (next to the old Marina Pier and Theatre – both since demolished) up to the promenade on the cliff top. Again, this shaft has long since disappeared, although two similar lifts still remain elsewhere along the seafront. As mentioned before, the lift further along from here, near the main sands, was in fact the first lift in Ramsgate. It has recently been renovated, and is used once again throughout the summer months.

Augusta Road, around 1905 and today. These two scenes are identical except for one obvious thing; the lack of cars in the original picture is quite striking compared to the modern view, which really demonstrates how the motor car has become such an important part of our lives.

This road is named after Lady Augusta Murray, daughter of the 4th Earl and Countess of Dunmore.

The small conical shaped building in the distance of both pictures is known as 'The Kiosk' on Victoria Parade, which has recently been restored. It was built around 1875 and its original purpose was to sell entry tickets for Victoria Gardens, which were accessed through a nearby turnstile, before they were purchased by the borough council.

This whole area of the East Cliff and its surrounding streets has changed very little in appearance over the past century, with its many Listed buildings and wonderful regency architecture surviving relatively intact.

View from the Eastcliff of Ramsgate in 1900 and today.

The East Cliff gives some fantastic views out to sea, especially during the Ramsgate Powerboat Grand Prix, which is now held here every summer. The modern picture shows the same view but with the tide out, revealing Ramsgate's main beach, which remained popular right up until the late 1960s, when the arrival of cheap international travel and foreign package holidays meant this beach, and hundreds more like it, became far less busy. However during the height of the summer season today, Ramsgate beach is still very popular – despite what the recent picture may show! – and has won many awards for its cleanliness.

Granville Hotel in 1901 and 2007. The Victorian shelter in the foreground is still there – again with a new coat of paint – but the bandstand and ornamental garden behind it have since been replaced by the Granville Theatre building, which still serves as a local cinema after many years. Only time will tell how the recent opening of a new ten-screen multiplex cinema at nearby Westwood Cross will affect its fortunes, and that of the other provincial cinemas located throughout the Isle of Thanet.

Wellington Crescent around 1900 and 2007. Clearly these two views have changed very little in the last century. Wellington Crescent has a beautiful row of Regency properties overlooking the sea, and the fine bandstand has recently undergone a complete restoration. Wellington Crescent was built on land used for barracks when Ramsgate was a garrison town during the Napoleonic Wars, and the surrounding streets, with names such as La Belle Alliance Square, Plains of Waterloo and Nelson Crescent were also built during that time, evoking memories of the Battle of Waterloo, and the role that Ramsgate played in this historic event.

East Cliff Promenade around 1900 and 2007. In the recent picture, this particular view is currently obscured by temporary fencing erected by Thanet District Council, when large cracks began to appear in the cliff. It is thought this subsidence is partly caused by the extensive underground caves and tunnels beneath Wellington Crescent, which were utilised by the Navy during the Second World War as air-raid shelters and ammunition stores which served two large gun emplacements on Wellington Crescent. Hopefully the cliff reinforcement work will be completed soon so this beautiful promenade can be restored back to its former glory.

Madeira Walk in 1908 and 2007. Madeira Walk is an attractive 'chine' which was cut out of the chalk to provide easy access to the harbour from the East Cliff. It is bordered on both sides by an artificial rockery designed by James Pulham and was officially opened on 6 April 1895. It is clear to see a lot more growth in the shrubbery here compared to last century, with the trees and bushes no longer cut back as much, but slowly taking over.

Corner of Madeira Walk, 1902 and 2007. Again, the trees and shrubbery are a lot higher now, obscuring the view out to sea. It does, however, make a nice haven for various types of birds in this tranquil spot, which makes a pleasant change from the usual seagulls.

ELECTRIC TRAM SMASH, RAMSGATE. AUG. 3rd 1905.

Another view of Madeira Walk from around 1901 and today. Again, the form of transport is very different. On 3 August 1905, a wet summer's day, a tram was making a routine descent of Madeira Walk hill, when suddenly it careered out of control, jumped the tracks, crashed through the railings and dropped over the 30ft cliff edge. Fortunately the few passengers travelling the tram that day came out of it unscathed, although the inexperienced driver sustained some injury. The trams continued to operate along this route until they were replaced by buses on 27 March 1937.

The Waterfall, Madeira Walk, around 1895 and 2007. These views are almost identical, but that is probably because water and rocks do not really change much over time! Note the ornate wooden bridge in the original picture has since been replaced with a stone one, most likely in the early 1900s. Interestingly, the original bridge shown here is also identical to the one crossing the lake in the early scenes from Ellington Park.

Construction started on Madeira Walk in 1892 at a cost of almost £60,000, although not many people realise that the rocks making up Madeira walk are entirely man made, from a substance called Pulhamite, and painted a sandstone colour. Similar artificial rockeries were also made in other parts of Ramsgate at that time, such as in Ellington Park (replacing the old lake) and also on the other side of Ramsgate, making up the attractive chine at the West Cliff.

Madeira Walk around 1902 and today. This view is looking down Madeira Walk hill, towards the harbour and seafront. In the original picture, a tram from the Electric Tramways and Lighting Co. Ltd can be seen labouring up the hill, negotiating the unique twists and adverse cambers of this hill.

The Peace Memorial, Albion place, around 1920 and 2006.

This memorial is called 'Destiny' and was unveiled by Dame Janet Stancomb-Wills to all the inhabitants of the town (including the animals). Contrary to the title on the original postcard, it is not a war memorial, but one of peace. It is completely untarnished by time and the monument remains identical to the original picture in every detail. Note how in the original photograph the bridge on the left (crossing above the waterfall) is now made of stone, rather than the wooden bridge shown in the earlier postcard of the waterfall on page 84.

Granville Hotel, *c.* 1900 and 2006. The ornamental garden guarded by the two lion statuettes to the right of the original picture is now the corner of the Granville Theatre (and cinema) shown to the right of the modern picture. The Granville Hotel was built by Edward Welby Pugin, oldest son of the famous architect Augustus Pugin, and was initially constructed as a row of large terraced houses, but were converted to a hotel shortly after, in 1869. Note the bust of Edward Pugin on the plinth in the foreground, and the two lion statuettes to the right. Similar lion statuettes also sit above the entrance to St Augustine's Abbey, another Pugin building (built by his father) on the Westcliff of Ramsgate, shown earlier in this book.

The Granville Hotel has since been converted back to residential apartments, after failing to recover its former grandeur as a hotel since being bombed in the Second World War. The lion statues still remain, although one has recently been removed by the council for repair after being vandalised.

The old Ramsgate Sands station, viewed from the Eastcliff, *c.* 1910 and 2008.

This is another view of the busy Ramsgate Harbour (Sands)Station, taken from the Eastcliff Promenade, and is looking in the opposite direction to the picture on page 34. Passengers would travel through a long chalk tunnel for over a mile, before emerging into the bright sunlight of Ramsgate Sands Station, where the trains terminated. When the station closed in 1926, the railway tunnel remained, and was put to good use as a narrow gauge 'scenic railway', until several bad chalk falls forced its closure in 1965.

The station site is now a building site (what remained of the station building burnt down in 1998), and scaffolding now completely obscures the modern view over the cliff edge. Very few traces remain of this once-busy railway terminus, although the blocked tunnel portal is still visible in the cliff face, with a steel door providing the only access into it. Also the circular outline of the original turntable is still there, although many people wouldn't realise what it once was!

The old photograph also provides an excellent view of the impressive Marina Pleasure Pier, sweeping out over the sea. This Promenade Pier was over 30ft wide and over 500ft long. As previously mentioned, it was demolished in 1930.

Winterstoke Gardens Pavilion, 1926 and 2006. This Pavilion is now quite a sorry sight compared to its original glory days. In its heyday in the 1920s and 1930s it was a pleasant spot to congregate and watch bands and concerts in the park. Those days are long gone and nowadays it is popular with the younger generation as an unofficial skate park, with the walls completely covered in graffiti. Since this picture was taken, the local council have made a great effort to clean it up, but seem to be facing a constant battle with the local graffiti artists and taggers to keep it clean.

Marina Gardens, East Cliff in 1905 and 2007. The Marina Theatre shown in the original postcard has long since disappeared, with a car park now in its place. Originally called the Marina Restaurant and Theatre of Varieties, interestingly British actor Sydney Greenstreet had his stage debut here playing a murderer in a 1902 production of *Sherlock Holmes*. He then went on to star in Hollywood films such as *The Maltese Falcon* before his death in 1954. This row of houses are built deep into the cliff face, and were originally Victorian holiday homes. The conical structures to the right of the old theatre mark the entrance to the Marina Pleasure Pier, demolished almost eighty years ago.

Lower Parade, East Cliff in 1901 and today. The skyline remains similar, although some of the old houses have been replaced by 1970s-style square ones. This row of houses were built into arches in the undercliff, and to the right of the modern houses there are still remains of derelict arches which were once houses similar to the ones shown in the postcard. The smaller of the arches were rumoured to have been small houses built especially for 'a troupe of midgets' who were a resident variety act at the adjacent Marina Theatre at one time, although this cannot be confirmed!

The 'New' East Cliff Promenade extension around 1905 and today.

At the beginning of the twentieth century Victoria Parade was extended so that the promenade could lead all the way up to what is now King George VI Memorial Park, which forms the border between Ramsgate's East Cliff and the neighbouring town of Broadstairs. This park was once the grounds of East Cliff Lodge, a remarkable gothic-style mansion built in 1799. In 1831 it was bought by the influential Jewish philanthropist Sir Moses Montefiore, who lived there until his death in 1885. The lodge was sadly demolished in 1954, and King George VI Memorial Park was created from the estate grounds. An attractive Italianate glass house still remains, however, and is currently being restored after suffering years of vandalism.

In the modern picture, a shelter has since been added and the gardens on the left of the original postcard were further landscaped in 1923, and became Winterstoke Gardens.

The San Clu Hotel, 1897 and 2007. This hotel was originally separate houses, known as Granville Terrace when they were originally constructed in 1882. These were then purchased in 1897 by an investor and converted to the Hotel Saint Cloud. The Hotel was sold in 1919, and the new owner renamed it San Clu. As you can see from the two pictures, half of the building is now missing. In October 1928 one side of the building was completely destroyed by fire. What is left of the San Clu has remained a hotel to this day, where it is now a Comfort Inn.

Wellington Crescent c.1901 and 2007. ... Wellington Crescent is a fine row of Regency houses overlooking the sea, on Ramsgate's East Cliff, built in the earlier part of the nineteenth century. There was once a fine oak statue of the Duke of Wellington erected in the middle of the lawn before it was burnt down (allegedly by a drunken Irishman!). It has since been replaced by a bandstand, which in 2006 had a major renovation.

Eastcliff Promenade in 1901 and today. This view is looking back towards Ramsgate harbour. When comparing the two pictures, it is evident how much land has been reclaimed from the sea over the last century. In the foreground, what was once a sandy beach (and later an open-air swimming pool) is now a car park. The Marina Pleasure Pier has also vanished (having been demolished in 1930). Marina Road remains unchanged, however, since it was opened in 1877. Regrettably, where the Marina Theatre proudly stood in the original picture is now just another overflow car park for the main beach (after a brief spell as a nightclub in the 1970s and 1980s). Perhaps the ever-increasing demand for parking spaces on the sea front is a good sign – that tourism is once again booming in Ramsgate, or perhaps, along with the closure of Ramsgate Sands Station, it just shows our ever-increasing dependence on the motor car?

Other local titles published by The History Press

Ramsgate and St Lawrence Revisited

DON DIMOND

This selection of over 200 archive images, many not published before, documents life in the busy seaside communities of Ramsgate and St Lawrence during 120 years. Events such as the Ramsgate Harbour Regatta and Peace Day celebrations in 1919 are recalled, alongside memorable characters, notable officials and beneficiaries who have helped to shape the area. Landmarks such as Ramsgate Harbour and the West Pier are also featured, making this a valuable history which will reawaken nostalgic memories.

978 07524 3868 9

Canterbury History You Can See

MARJORIE LYLE

This detailed history of Canterbury is told through its buildings from its Roman origins to the present day and includes sections on St Martin's church, St Augustine's Abbey, the Cathedral and Precincts, the Pilgrim Inns, Royal Castle, timber-framed and Georgian houses, the Blitz, shopping malls and universities. The reader is introduced to the builders, traders, craftsmen and saints and sinners who created Canterbury during its long history and tells many surprising stories about the people behind the buildings creating an informative and entertaining read.

978 07624 4538 0

The Kent Downs

DAN TUSON

Nestled within the heart of the county, sparsely settled and largely untouched by the pressures of the modern age, the Kent Downs are home to some of the most enchanting countryside in southern England. Richly illustrated with over 100 stunning photographs in colour and monochrome, the book is a tribute to the many who have found solace and inspiration in the Kent Downs and will appeal to all those who visit, work or live in this cherished part of the county of Kent.

978 07524 4405 5

Who's Buried Where In Kent

ALAN MAJOR

This fascinating book will leave you humbled and uplifted. Within its pages the reader will discover the famous, infamous, notable, curious and eccentric people who were buried in Kent's churches, churchyards and cemeteries. From the grave of a soldier who won the Victoria Cross for rescuing comrades from cannibals, to a ninety-year-old spinster who died 'with all her faculties', there are also many graves of heroes and heroines, pioneers, inventors, poets, artists, sportsmen, politicians, royalty and even smugglers!

978 07524 4544 1

If you are interested in purchasing other books published by The History Press, or in case you have difficulty finding any History Press books in your local bookshop, you can also place orders directly through our website

www.thehistorypress.co.uk